I Like Giving.®

THE 7 WAYS OF LIVING GENEROUSLY

Give, share, and show you care.

 GENEROUS THOUGHTS: Use a thought in my mind to think something kind.

 GENEROUS WORDS: Use what I say to make someone's day.

 GENEROUS MONEY: Use my money — no matter how much — if there is a life I can touch.

 GENEROUS TIME: Use any moment in my day to put Generosity on display.

 GENEROUS INFLUENCE: Use the choices that I make to affect the actions other people take.

 GENEROUS ATTENTION: Use my eyes to look and ears to hear. Listen well and distractions disappear.

 GENEROUS BELONGINGS: Use what I have to share — I can do this anywhere.

Marco the Monkey and the Marvelous Money

Copyright © 2024 by I Like Giving.®

Author Betta Tugive is the pen name for the I Like Giving.® Writing Team.

Scriptures taken from the Holy Bible, New International Version®, NIV®. Copyright © 1973, 1978, 1984, 2011 by Biblica, Inc.™ Used by permission of Zondervan. All rights reserved worldwide. www.zondervan.com. The "NIV" and "New International Version" are trademarks registered in the United States Patent and Trademark Office by Biblica, Inc.™

All rights reserved. No part of this book may be reproduced or transmitted in any form or by any means, electronic or mechanical, including photocopying and recording, or by information storage or retrieval system, without permission in writing from I Like Giving.®

Printed in the United States of America 2024.

ISBN 979-8-9880723-5-5

**Dedicated to Harold and Sue —
big-hearted givers.**

I Like Giving.® Writing Team:
S.F. Aughtmon
and friends

Illustrated by
Ben Cole & Andy Towler

Story inspired by NorthPointe Christian Schools

Special thanks to the Hartshorn family

The Giving Adventure Series

**Jasper G and the
Me-Thinking Madness**

**Ellie the Elephant and the
Stinkin' Thinkin'**

**Polly the Parrot and the
Wonderful Words**

**Marco the Monkey and the
Marvelous Money**

MARCO THE MONKEY
AND THE
MARVELOUS MONEY

BY

Betta Tugive

I Like Giving. Publishing
Colorado Springs, CO

In the land of the givers, where sharing is cool,
lived a marvelous saver who showed up for school.
Marco looked for his pal, sang a shy little song,

"I've been saving my pennies. Yep, all summer long —

for the Fill-A-Jar Rally that's held every year. I can't wait to get in on what's happening here."

"Same for me!"

came a bellow from Leroy, his friend.

"And with all of our cash, they'll have plenty to spend."

Marco placed both his jars near the basketball booth.

"Those old courts are worn out, and we know that's the truth."

BEAUTIFY THE BASKETBALL COURTS

"All the giving's amazing. We're doing our part!"
Leroy's generous words filled his monkey-shaped heart.

"Now you'll see all the backboards and nets will be new.
And you'll hear every swish
when your free throws go through."

Leroy added his jar.

I've been growing a lot,
so I got a new chair.
Yes, it's great, but I know
I can't get over there.

All the fun's far away.
But now what can I do?
'Cuz this bridge is too narrow.
My chair can't squeeze through.

**Sure, I want to join in.
I don't like to complain.**

Then a lion-sized tear rolled down into his mane.

Marco's heart gave a thump —
a new feeling broke through —
a big **DO-SOMETHING** feeling!
But what could he do?

Then his heart got his thinker to notice the truth.

Could it be that my jars
 are not at the right booth?
I've been saving for me,
 for the game I adore.
Yes, I love playing hoops,
 but I love my friend more.

*Maybe others can help,
now that I've made my choice.
Oh, I'll give with my heart,
and I'll speak with my voice!*

Marco's voice shook a bit.

"Everybody, look here."

Then his whisper grew louder.

"There's one thing that's clear."

"Everybody can play on the slide and the swing!
But our pal Leroy can't —
and that's just the worst thing!"

"So let's fix that old bridge, and let's give with our hearts. Bring your jars over here. This is right where it starts."

All the friends gathered round bringing jars upon jars. Marco took a deep breath as he reached for the stars.

"We don't have quite enough, but we'll figure it out and make marvelous money!" he said with a shout.

"So let's all keep on saving. There's more we can share. Can't we give our friend more than a bridge for his chair?"

Leroy's class was all in, filling jars way up high.
For a year they sold cupcakes and fresh apple pie.

And they all went to work as they rolled up their sleeves.
Yes, they cut neighbors' lawns, and they raked up their leaves.

Then another class gave,
then the whole school came through!

A love-ripple-effect had changed their thinkers too!

When the big day arrived, all the kids gave a cheer! Leroy yelled, "Everyone! Our new playground is here!"

Say, would you do the same,

and speak up for a friend?

Let your **DO-SOMETHING** feeling

change up how you spend?

It's a marvelous thing when
you give from the heart.
A love-ripple-effect will
grow fast once you start!

Talk About It!

Why do you think that Marco decided to give his money jar to help Leroy?

What do you think a DO-SOMETHING feeling is?

Is there a special project in your community that your family could give toward?

Giving Challenge

Fill-A-Jar Challenge
Designate a jar where your family members can place coins and money they want to share when a giving opportunity comes up.

DO-SOMETHING Challenge
Look for ways you can show Generosity and then **DO SOMETHING!** Tag @generousfamily and tell us about it!

And do not forget to do good and to share with others, for with such sacrifices God is pleased.
Hebrews 13:16 (NIV)

Visit **generouskidsbookclub.com** to get Marco's story, meet our other Jungle Friends, and join our monthly book club!

GENEROUS STUDENTS
HOMESCHOOL EDITION

Join the Generosity Road Trip! **Generous Students™: Homeschool Edition** explores The 7 Ways of Living Generously for all age groups!

generousfamily.com

Check out our K-8 faith-based, biblical SEL curriculum! Generous Classroom™ is sharing the importance of gratitude and teaching the next generation how to be life-long givers!

K-2

3-5

6-8

generousclassroom.com